MURPHY goes to CHURCH

BY STEVE DENNIE
and ROB SUGGS

INTERVARSITY PRESS
DOWNERS GROVE, ILLINOIS 60515

InterVarsity Press® is the book-publishing division of InterVarsity Christian Fellowship®, a student movement active on campus at hundreds of universities, colleges and schools of nursing in the United States of America, and a member movement of the International Fellowship of Evangelical Students. For information about local and regional activities, write Public Relations Dept., InterVarsity Christian Fellowship, 6400 Schroeder Rd., P.O. Box 7895, Madison, WI 53707-7895.

Cover illustration: Rob Suggs

ISBN 0-8308-1837-5

Printed in the United States of America ∞

Library of Congress Cataloging-in-Publication Data
Dennie, Steve, 1956-
    Murphy goes to church/Steve Dennie and Rob Suggs.
      p.   cm.
    ISBN 0-8308-1837-5
    1. Christian life—Humor.   2. Christian life—Caricatures and
cartoons.   3. American wit and humor, Pictorial.   4. Murphy's law.
5. Murphy's law—Caricatures and cartoons.   I. Suggs, Rob.
II. Title.
BV4517.D46   1993
250'.207—dc20   93-18096
                                          CIP

17	16	15	14	13	12	11	10	9	8	7	6	5	4	3	2	1
06	05	04	03	02	01	00	99	98	97	96	95	94	93			

Contents

Introduction

Like most people who grew up in Sunday school, we were taught "All things work together for good." That's how King James put it. Newer Bible translations render Romans 8:28 a little differently, and probably more accurately. But we still prefer "All things work together for good." It's very comforting when things go awry. Which is what Murphy's Law is all about!

The original Murphy's Law says, "If anything can go wrong, it will." Hundreds of laws, axioms, corollaries, principles and theorems have arisen around Mr. Murphy's original observation.

☐ Nothing is as easy as it looks.
☐ Everything takes longer than you think.
☐ The other line always moves faster.
☐ When things can't get any worse, they will.

Murphy's Law reigns in the Real World, inflicting itself on us in numerous ways. At home. At work. At play. And at church. Yes, Murphy not only attends church, but he's a very active member. This book shows him in action.

Fortunately, Romans 8:28 serves pretty much as an anti-Murphy's Law. No matter how many things go wrong, we can anticipate a happy ending of some kind. But *before* all things work together for good, Murphy takes his shots.

Steve Dennie and Rob Suggs

1 / Murphy in His Pew

The Law of Inopportune Wailing

Saying "Let us pray" causes babies to cry.

Altar Call Corollary:
So does singing "Just as I am."

Commentary:
The number of crying babies increases geometrically with each verse.

The Conspicuous Certitude

If you sit up front, there's more chance that:

☐ You'll be called to the nursery because your child just threw up.

☐ Your beeper will go off, probably during a prayer.

☐ You'll get a phone call.

☐ A lady with towering hair will sit in front of you.

- [ ] You'll fall asleep during the sermon.
- [ ] Nature will call.
- [ ] You cut yourself shaving that morning, and the blood is dripping down the back of your neck.
- [ ] Your baby will cry.

The Man's Job Notion

Women cannot serve as ushers.

Corollary:
Nobody knows why.

Law of the Inevitable Slump

Just when attendance picks up, summer arrives.

The Unwritten Law of Squatter's Rights

Sitting in a pew three consecutive Sundays is nine-tenths of ownership.

The Latecomer's Lament

The last seats to be filled are in the middle of the front pews.

Heather's Purple Prescription

The lighter the color of the sanctuary carpet, the greater the chance people will spill communion juice.

The Droning Author Warning

You can't tell a guest speaker by his book.

The Minimalist Motto

Any service would be more effective with:
- ☐ One less sermon point
- ☐ One less song
- ☐ One less announcement
- ☐ One less prayer

THE · TO - EVERY - EXCUSE · THERE · IS · A · SEASON PRINCIPLE:

IN AUTUMN THEY'RE GONE TO SEE THE LEAVES.

IN WINTER IT'S TOO NASTY TO GO OUTSIDE.

IN SPRING IT'S TOO NICE TO SIT INSIDE.

IN SUMMER THEY'RE AT THE LAKE...

The Standing on the Pinnacles Principle

The higher the average length of women's high heels, the longer the pastoral prayer.

Corollary:
The longer the pastoral prayer, the more likely the congregation will be asked to stand.

The Theory of the Familiar Palm Tree

Missionaries all use the same set of slides.

The Law of Celebrity Delinquency

If you visit a church to hear a famous preacher, he will be gone that Sunday.

The Two-Timer's Rule

Here today, gone until Easter.

The Sick Kid Alibi

The more children you have, the more excuses you have for skipping church.

The Bakker & Co. Admonition

Trust everybody, but have two people count the offering.

The Law of the Ingathering

The service's actual starting time is ten minutes after the announced starting time.

Corollary:
Everyone in the congregation knows this.

The Laws of Uncertain Origins

If you arrive early, the service will start late.
If you arrive late, the service will have started early.

The Proximity Postulate

Members living fifteen miles away will be early. Members living two houses away will be late.

The Early Bird Rule: Fools rush in . . . and get the back pews.

The Evangelistically Speaking Equation

Actual Attendance: n.

Attendance as reported to the board: $n + 5$.

Attendance as reported to the denomination: $n + 10$.

Attendance as reported in the district pastors' meeting: $n + 20$.

Attendance as counted by the ushers: $n - 10$.

Laws of the Perpetual Recession

When the economy is bad, people give less.

When the economy is good, people give less.

Anthony's Observation

The more uncomfortable the pews, the longer the sermon.

Extension:

If the pews are padded, you will be asked to stand through most of the service.

The Thief-in-the-Night Principle

The year's lowest attendance occurs when the district superintendent makes a surprise visit.

Laws of Sound Systems

Testing the PA system before the service causes it to malfunction during the service.

The more expensive your sound system, the more likely it will break down.

Finding a professional sound technician to run the system increases the likelihood of malfunctions.

If you say "Is this on?"—it is.

The Off-Sunday Rule

Visitors are most likely to come when you have:

☐ A congregational meeting.
☐ A stewardship drive.
☐ A Gideon speaker.
☐ Communion.
☐ An electrical failure.

The Visitor's Rule

When in doubt, stay seated.

The Miraculous Disappearance Theory

Several short books completely vanish from your Bible when you are asked to stand and read from them.

The Styrofoam-of-Life Suspicion

If communion wafers were made of Styrofoam, no one would notice the difference.

The "Where's the Bathroom?" Rule

Church visitors will ask other visitors for directions.

2/ Murphy on the Board

The Multiple Choice

When presented with several optional dates for a special church event, the board will pick the one which conflicts with a Women's Fellowship meeting (and we all know who will win that battle).

Pam's Principle

In the treasurer's report, the only mistake is the number which everyone agrees is obviously right.

Ray's Rule of Follow-Through

After a weekend board retreat during which members establish a five-year master plan with detailed goals, concrete objectives, and specific dates for implementation and evaluation, the members will ignore the plan and carry on as usual.

Gideon's Principle of Delayed Action

The arguments for referring a motion to the pastoral staff for further study are always better than the arguments for taking a vote.

The Reshuffle Fallacy

Spiritual problems can be solved by reorganizing the administrative structure.

The Caffeine and Calories Prescription

Attendance at meetings increases if cookies and coffee are served.

The Law of Tangents

The more trivial the subject, the more the board will discuss it.

Corollary:
The more eternal the need, the less attention it gets.

Corollary:
80% of the time will be spent discussing property issues.

Corollary:
Spiritual matters are voted on with little discussion.

Corollary:
Constantly discussing a spiritual need causes it to disappear.

The Law of the Hired Scapegoat

If a committee makes a bad decision, nobody will be blamed—unless the pastor is a member.

The Democratic Disadvantage

For any church position, people will elect the least-qualified person.

Saul's Law of Infallible Selection

A pastoral search committee can be wrong, but never in doubt.

Corollary:
In any pastoral search, the best candidate will preach the worst trial sermon.

The Secretary Prerequisite

Men always expect female committee members to take minutes.

3 / Murphy Sings Bass

The Back-Seat Singer Law

Behind every good songleader is a pastor singing the wrong verse.

Corollary:
And singing it loud.

Corollary:
And an accompanist playing too slow.

The Fourth-as-the-Last Routine

Christians sing some verses all of the time, and all verses some of the time, but not all verses all of the time.

The Barrows Addition:
Except during altar calls.

The Wing-It Rule

The words printed in the hymnal and being sung by the songleader never match exactly.

Extension:
When songleaders pause between verses to talk, they resume singing in a different key.

The Law of Hymnal Revision

When you finally get used to the idiosyncrasies in the denominational hymnal, they publish a new one.

Corollary:
The new hymnal either omits your favorite hymns or sets them to strange tunes you've never heard before.

The Pianist's Complaint

Accompanists won't find out about changes in hymn numbers until after they play the introduction to the wrong hymn.

Aaron's Amen Assertions

When the organist plays the "Amen" at the end of a hymn, the people don't sing it.

When the people do sing the "Amen," the organist doesn't play it.

If you tell people whether or not they are supposed to sing the "Amen," they forget by the second verse.

The Mucho Vibrato Principle

The church's worst soloist will want to sing "O Holy Night" in the Christmas program.

The Baritone Advantage

He who sings the loudest determines which verse the congregation sings next.

The Familiarity Factor

The more you sing a particular hymn, the less people notice the words.

The Gaping Hole Inevitability

Someone sitting in the choir loft behind the pastor will yawn throughout the service.

First Law of the Choir

You need one more copy of the music.

Second Law of the Choir

Absent choir members all sing the same part.

Third Law of the Choir

The soprano soloist will contract laryngitis the day before the Christmas cantata.

Jerry's Contention

We're not flat. The organ's sharp.

Devonshire's Rule of Special Music

Visiting singers speak longer than the pastor.

The Law of Musical Entropy

When left by themselves, carefully numbered accompaniment tapes rearrange themselves so as to cause maximum confusion.

Corollary:
The wrong tape has the label of the tape you're looking for.

4 / Murphy Saves the World

The Uttermost Parts Principle

Compassion for the lost increases with distance.

Corollary:
If they live next door, they don't need your concern.

Russ's Observation

Car problems, working overtime, traffic congestion and headaches increase on visitation night.

Law of the Tent Meeting

When an evangelistic strategy stops being effective, seminaries will build a required course around it.

Don's Law of Visitation

House numbers are never illuminated or large enough to read.

Janet's Addition:
If you can read the number, it's the wrong house.

The Law of Lost Sheep

All church prospects live in new subdivisions not on the map.

The Law of Testimonies

People listen much more closely when you talk about your non-Christian days.

Corollary:
The greatest saints have the most boring testimonies.

The Law of Stray Sheep

People you witness to for three years will get saved when someone else witnesses to them.

Corollary:
People who get saved in your church live next door to another church.

Lamport's Law of Sanctified Hydrophobia

Non-Christians who fear water will be converted in churches that practice baptism by immersion.

Corollary:
The more overweight people are, the more likely they are to insist on being baptized by immersion.

The Law of Seeking and Not Finding: Door-to-door visitation is enjoyed most when the prospective church members aren't home.

The Weak Moment Rule

The stupid driver you honk at will sit beside you in church next Sunday.

Joanne's Dictum

When you plan an evangelistic outreach event, only Christians attend.

5 / Murphy Adds On

The Multiple Chefs Analogy

The fewer people on the building committee, the quicker, cheaper, better and more efficiently the work will get done.

The Recession Hypothesis

Starting a capital fund drive causes massive job layoffs in the community.

Bob's First Rule of Construction

A building committee will choose the options which will have the most delays and cost over-runs.

Corollary:
Any wise choice will be overruled by the board.

Bob's Second Rule of Construction

All hours of labor pledged to the building project must be divided by three.

Bob's Third Rule of Construction

Materials needed first arrive two weeks late.

Corollary:
Inquiring about the delay causes the materials to be back-ordered indefinitely.

The Edifice Complex Principle

Simple revisions made during construction will add up to an irreparable design flaw.

The Bigger Barn Rule

No matter how large the new building, it will be one room short.

6 / Murphy Eats Roast Preacher

The Judas Axiom

People act most positive toward the pastor just before asking for a resignation.

The Forty Pieces of Silver Postulate

The larger the Christmas gift, the less the congregation likes the pastor. (They figure the pastor will need the money for moving expenses.)

The Law of Just Deserts

Griping pastors attract griping laypeople.

Corollary:
The pastor's greatest critics in the congregation will be the most faithful attenders.

Corollary:
The pastor's strongest critic will be elected board chair.

The What-You-See Conclusion

The pastor only works two hours a week.

The TV Preacher Antithesis

The pastor always needs a new suit.

Corollary:
If the pastor can afford a new suit, he's obviously overpaid.

The Revolving Door Dictum

Nothing is so bad that it can't be made worse by changing pastors.

When-Push-Comes-to-Shove Corollary:
It's easier to change pastors than to change laypeople.

The Blame-the-Other-Guy Convenience

The previous pastor will be blamed for everything wrong in the church, until the successor leaves.

Law of the Squeaky Parishioner

The feedback the pastor receives is the opposite of the congregation's general feeling on the issue.

7 / Murphy Gets Ordained

The Three Laws of Parsonage Life

Parishioners call only at mealtime.

Two weeks before the new parsonage is completed, you'll be moved to a different church.

Parishioners regard the parsonage as public property.

The Perfect Parent Problem

Pastors must create quality family time between midnight and six a.m.

The Holy Terror Law

All mischief can be traced to the preacher's kids.

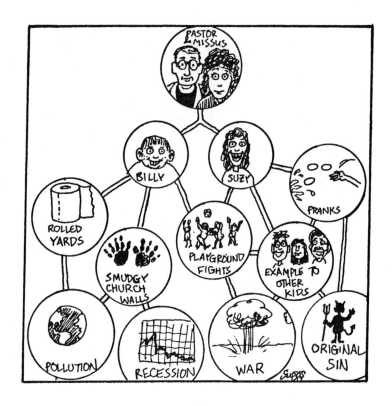

The Filibuster Syndrome

In any district pastors' meeting, the pastors who talk the most about what's happening in their churches have the least happening.

The Vacation Expectation

"Pillars" of the church only die when the pastor is on vacation.

The Last Shall Be First Law

The pastor is the last person to know and the first to get blamed.

The Crying Shoulder Syndrome

The length of the counseling session is inversely proportional to the problem.

The Tenure Principle

Those who can't pastor, pastor many churches.

The Girth Factor

The bigger they are, the smaller the pulpit.

The Keep-'Em-Humble Contention

The bigger the church, the smaller the office.

The Law of Pastoral Leadership

When you're right, it must have been the Lord's leading. When you're wrong, you've got communication problems with the Almighty.

Corollary:
To err is unspiritual.

The Domino Principle

Ineffective pastors multiply ineffective churches.

The Law of Unpaid Dues

Those who can grow churches, do.

Those who can't grow churches lead church growth seminars.

Clarification:
Monkey see, monkey teach others to do

The Mission Field Simulation

If you grew up in the city, your first church will be in the country.

The Best Laid Plans Principle

Printing the names of staff persons on new letterhead causes a staff change.

8 / Murphy Teaches Sunday School

Lamport's Theory of Last-Minute Preparation

The farther the teachers live from the church, the better prepared they will be upon arriving.

The Helpmeet Rule

The year's largest Sunday-school attendance will come on the day your helper is sick.

Laws of Purchased Creativity

More Laws of Purchased Creativity

The more closely you follow the teacher's quarterly, the less students will like it.

The more expensive the materials, the less the students will like them.

On any given Sunday, the absent students are the only ones who took a quarterly home the previous week.

On Saturday night, you'll remember that last Sunday's substitute still has the teacher's quarterly.

Extension:
That person left on vacation yesterday.

Lange's Law of the Chalkboard

You never have enough chalk to actually hold.

Corollary:
The only available chalk is a fluorescent purple that only shows up under black light.

The AV Axiom

When one teacher needs to use the church's only overhead projector, so does another teacher.

The Law of the Thorn-Covered Rose

Good content plus lousy teaching equals lousy teaching.

The Janitor's Admonition

Never leave crayons and toddlers alone together.

The Law of Close Fellowship

The larger the class, the smaller its room.

The Rambler's Reality

The more the teacher talks, the less students learn.

9 / Murphy Tries Church Growth

The Law of Program Predictability

If you don't expect a program to work, it won't.

If you do expect a program to work, it won't.

If you decide to eliminate a program, it will suddenly become effective.

The Bishop's Bane

If headquarters recommends it, it won't work in your church.

The Ultimate Rationale

If it doesn't work, it wasn't God's will.

The Law of Institutionalization

Ministries become less fruitful with time.

Corollary:
Ministries also become indestructible with time.

Corollary:
Traditions not only die hard, they eventually become immortal.

The All Things Dictum

A ministry designed to reach all age groups won't significantly minister to any age group.

The Law of Misplaced Saints

The people best qualified to work in a particular ministry are already involved in a ministry for which they are unqualified.

The Statute of Imitations

What works at the megachurch won't work for you.

Corollary:
Success breeds failures.

Freddy Freeloader's Commentary

Every inactive member has an idea that will work.

The Good Ol' Days Remembrance

Nostalgia is the refuge of the stagnant.

The Naysayers Tip-Off

People who normally oppose change go along with changes destined to fail.

The Rut Constant

People don't oppose change. They only oppose bad ideas.

Corollary:
Change is a bad idea.

Rules of Ministry Engagement

If you have the money to support a program, you don't have enough volunteers.

If you have enough volunteers, you don't have enough money.

If you have enough volunteers and money, it will definitely flop.

The Money-Where-Your-Mouth-Is Principle

Fools and their ideas are soon appointed.

The Law of Vanishing Resources

The only person who knows where last year's Vacation Bible School materials are stored died last March.

The Law of Religious Inferiority

No matter what the church does, someone will say that the business world does it better.

The Shepherd-Stealing Axiom

If your church grows, another church will steal your pastor at the height of your momentum.

The Ivory Tower Declaration

Whatever headquarters recommends, successful churches aren't doing.

10 / Murphy Works with Youth

Mark's Worst Scenario

The snow blizzard of the decade will occur at the end of the all-night lock-in, preventing parents from picking up their kids until the next day.

The Straying Sheep Inevitability

Don't play hide-and-seek at the youth group overnight. Some of the kids won't be found for days.

Stenner's Forecast

Whenever you schedule a youth car wash, it will rain.

Christy's Law of Lasting Impressions

The time you accidentally use a permanent marker on the white board, will be during the annual "sex talk."

Cheryl's Law of Inverted Supervision

If the majority of adult volunteers are male, the majority of teens will be female.

Law of Incongruent Affinity

Adults volunteer as youth sponsors in inverse proportion to their ability to relate to youth.

Blair's Rules of Parallel Inadequacy

Youth ministers are people too immature to be pastors.

Pastors are people too immature to be youth ministers.

Yeascott's Laws of Youth Work

Those who can do youth ministry are already committed to leading junior church.

People who can't do youth ministry present "how-to" seminars.

The Rule of the Usual Suspects

If something breaks, blame it on the youth group.

Corollary:

If it isn't the youth group's fault, then it's not broken. Some wise board member wanted the window to look that way.

Youth Director Prerequisites

Young equals qualified.

Young equals inexperienced and immature.

Therefore, qualified equals inexperienced and immature.

The Florida Axiom

The longer the distance, the greater the number of mechanical breakdowns on the church bus.

Corollary:
The church van never breaks down within fifteen miles of the church.

11 / Murphy Gets Over- Involved

Church Veteran's Woe

Even if you say no when asked to volunteer, you'll end up doing it anyway.

The Law of Congregational Default

The smaller the staff, the greater the need for volunteers.

The greater the need for volunteers, the greater the chance the pastor will have to do it.

Five Truths of Church Potlucks

For any potluck, you always need one more table.

The more time you spend preparing a dish for the church potluck, the less people will like it.

The line on the other side of the table always moves faster.

A potluck will outdraw Billy Graham any day of the week.

The number of people at the noon potluck will exceed the number of people in the morning service.

The Pass It On Principle

It only takes a hayride to get a spark going.

The Matchmaker's Delight

Singles retreats lead to larger marriage enrichment retreats.

The First Rule of Christmas Programs

Don't even think about using real sheep.

The Goodies Principle

For any fellowship event, you need one more pack of cookies.

Corollary:
Buying too many cookies causes attendance to decrease.

The Tribulation Worketh Endurance Postulate

The more things go wrong at the wedding, the longer the marriage will last.

The Invisible Man Truism

The father of the groom might as well not exist.

Prayer Meeting Postulates

If you discuss a prayer concern but don't explain it to God in an actual prayer, God won't know what you want.

If the prayer doesn't begin with "Dear Lord and Precious Heavenly Father," it will get sent to the wrong address.

The False Advertising Strategy

Church workdays would be better attended if called "fellowship dinners."

Fellowship dinners would be better attended if called "bowling night."

Committee meetings would be better attended if called "church workdays."

Extension:
Anything would be better attended if called a "potluck."

First Law of Church Athletics

Softball players and their Christianity are soon parted.

Second Law of Church Athletics

Increasing the number of Christians on the church softball team causes a proportional increase in the amount of arguing.

Third Law of Church Athletics

A church with a spotless image is a church without athletic teams.

Fourth Law of Church Athletics

Where there is a church basketball game, sin is not absent.

The Goliath Principle

Carnal churches have the tallest basketball players.

Laws of the Nursery

Mothers of infants never want to work in the nursery.

Nursery workers are always available last week.

The diapers a mother leaves with her infant will go on other infants.

Law of Bible Studies

People with the shallowest insights
dominate discussion.

12 / Murphy in the Pulpit

First Law of Sermons

The longer it takes to prepare a sermon, the less people will remember it.

Corollary:
The sermon you threw together at the last minute will be a big hit.

Second Law of Sermons

If you thought you just preached a great sermon, you'll soon be told differently.

Third Law of Sermons

Spending twice the normal amount of time preparing the sermon causes it to bomb.

Fourth Law of Sermons

If you're sure you have never used a certain sermon illustration with that audience, you have.

Fifth Law of Sermons

The sermon point which you consider most important will have to be cut because it breaks the alliterative scheme.

Sixth Law of Sermons

A hastily prepared, unrehearsed sermon will run ten minutes longer than the time allotted.

Corollary:
A carefully planned and rehearsed sermon will run twenty minutes overtime.

Seventh Law of Sermons

Sermons expand to fill all available time.

Corollary:
And then some.

Eighth Law of Sermons

The best sermon illustrations are the ones that embarrass your wife.

Predictable Extension:
You'll wish you had cleared it with her first.

Ninth Law of Sermons

The conclusion is the place in sermon preparation that the pastor reached on Saturday night.

Tenth Law of Sermons

There is no correlation between attending preaching seminars and preaching good sermons.

Corollary:
Uneducated ministers tend to be the most interesting.

The Law of Total Annihilation

Today's FATAL ERROR— UNRECOVERABLE DATA is tomorrow's sermon.

Blair's Law of Eternal Oblivion

The electricity will blink off just before you hit "save."

The Eutychus Principle

People fall asleep during sermons for a reason.

The Law of Exposed Ignorance

If you pretend to speak on a subject with authority, a real authority will attend that day.

The Preacher's Perplexion

Jesus never alliterated.

The Law of the Unknown Source

When in doubt, cite Spurgeon.

The Bluffer's Refuge

You can get away with anything by saying, "According to the original Greek . . ."

Commentary on Alliterative Futility: When all five points of the sermon begin with the same letter, people don't even remember the letter.

More-Is-Less Observations

The more profound the sermon, the less interesting it is.

The longer the sermon series, the less people like it.

The more intriguing the sermon title, the less interesting it will be.

The longer the sermon, the less chance people will remember it.

Corollary:
There is no such thing as a brief sermon.

The Peter Preacher Principle

Those who can preach, preach.

Those who can't preach teach homiletics in seminary.

Those who can't teach homiletics write books about it which are used as texts by homiletics professors.

The Sermon Barrel Contention

Pastors only preach what God has laid on their hearts.

Corollary:
God frequently uses old sermons.

The Law of Confused Origins

Nobody really cares how Webster defines a word found in the Bible.

The Parable Principle

People will remember the illustration, but not the application.

The Fact of the Ignored Hint

Placing a clock in the back of the sanctuary directly in the pastor's line of sight doesn't make a bit of difference.

The Overtime Rule

At noon, people turn off their ears.

The Apocryphal Truism

"The story is told . . ." means it never happened.

The Hair Spray Indication

There is a direct correlation between the amount of frenzied pacing and the size of the hairdo.

The You-Asked-For-It Warning

Preaching about marriage increases the amount of crisis marital counseling.

13 / Murphy Gets the Word Out

The First Rule of Announcementology

Any carefully worded announcement can be interpreted several different ways, none of them compatible with the intended meaning.

The Second Rule of Announcementology

The most important announcement stands the greatest chance of getting left out of the bulletin.

Corollary:
People who *never* read the bulletin will look for that particular announcement.

The Third Rule of Announcementology

The length of an announcement is inversely proportional to the number of people it affects.

The Fourth Rule of Announcementology

If it's not mentioned in the bulletin, it won't happen.

Corollary:
If the bulletin doesn't mention Christmas, people will assume it's been canceled.

The Fifth Rule of Announcementology

Nobody reads the bulletin.

The Sixth Rule of Announcementology

Decreasing the number of bulletins causes a proportional increase in attendance.

The Seventh Rule of Announcementology

A bulletin that contains no errors when copied Saturday afternoon will mysteriously develop typos overnight.

The Eighth Rule of Announcementology

The bulletin mentions me, therefore I am.

The Appointed Rounds Exception

A mailing about a special Saturday-night event will be delivered the following Monday.

The Law of Overkill

If you're an editor for *USA Today*, you'll be asked to do the church's photocopied newsletter.

The Rule of Thumb for Mission Board Obsolescence

In any bulletin board display of your denomination's missionaries, one-third of the missionaries no longer serve as missionaries, and another third are dead.

Corollary:
The uglier the bulletin board, the longer it stays up.

The Madalyn Murray O'Hair Postulate

Rumors are indestructible.

The Law of Theological Fog

The length and verbosity of the pastor's answer is inversely related to how well he or she understands your question.

The Law of Irreconcilable Operating Systems

It's easier for a camel to go through the eye of a needle than for a MacIntosh and a DOS person to enter heaven side by side.

The Dennie/Suggs Camel-Threading Corollary:
Or to do a book together.

The Church Library Observation

Books written after 1940 aren't allowed in the church library.

The Armageddon Observation

Those who don't learn from the past are condemned to write end-times books.

Corollary:
God doesn't read prophecy books.

The Inevitable Return

This book has given you many glimpses of Murphy in action. But there's much more to this insidious fellow than has met our eyes. You can no doubt provide further insights into how Murphy torments the saints. Please send us your own laws, corollaries, extensions and rules showing Mr. Murphy's influence on the church and Christian living. You may find your contribution in a future collection of Murphy's laws.

Send to: Murphy Goes to Church Editor
           InterVarsity Press
           P.O. Box 1400
           Downers Grove, IL 60515